Monthly Budget Planner

All Rights Reserved.

All rights reserved. No part of this publications may be reproduced, distributed, or transmitted in any form or by any means, including photocopying, recording, other electronic, or mechanical methods.

Sections

1. Debt Tracker
2. Monthly Expense Log
3. My Financial Goals
4. Savings Trackers
5. My Assets
6. Financial Year in Review
7. Finance Notes

Debt Tracker

It's time to analyze my debt to determine where I stand

What are my loans and credit cards?
What are the account numbers?
When are the payments due?
What are the interest rates?
What are the payoff dates?

Debt Tracker

CREDITOR

ACCOUNT NUMBER

STARTING BALANCE

CREDIT LIMIT

TARGET PAYOFF DATE

CREDIT TYPE

MINIMUM PAYMENT

INTEREST DATE

DATE	MINIMUM PAYMENT	AMOUNT PAID	BALANCE	NOTES

Debt Tracker

CREDITOR
ACCOUNT NUMBER
STARTING BALANCE
CREDIT LIMIT

TARGET PAYOFF DATE
CREDIT TYPE
MINIMUM PAYMENT
INTEREST DATE

DATE	MINIMUM PAYMENT	AMOUNT PAID	BALANCE	NOTES

Debt Tracker

CREDITOR

ACCOUNT NUMBER

STARTING BALANCE

CREDIT LIMIT

TARGET PAYOFF DATE

CREDIT TYPE

MINIMUM PAYMENT

INTEREST DATE

DATE	MINIMUM PAYMENT	AMOUNT PAID	BALANCE	NOTES

Debt Tracker

CREDITOR

ACCOUNT NUMBER

STARTING BALANCE

CREDIT LIMIT

TARGET PAYOFF DATE

CREDIT TYPE

MINIMUM PAYMENT

INTEREST DATE

DATE	MINIMUM PAYMENT	AMOUNT PAID	BALANCE	NOTES

Debt Tracker

CREDITOR

ACCOUNT NUMBER

STARTING BALANCE

CREDIT LIMIT

TARGET PAYOFF DATE

CREDIT TYPE

MINIMUM PAYMENT

INTEREST DATE

DATE	MINIMUM PAYMENT	AMOUNT PAID	BALANCE	NOTES

Debt Tracker

CREDITOR

ACCOUNT NUMBER

STARTING BALANCE

CREDIT LIMIT

TARGET PAYOFF DATE

CREDIT TYPE

MINIMUM PAYMENT

INTEREST DATE

DATE	MINIMUM PAYMENT	AMOUNT PAID	BALANCE	NOTES

Debt Tracker

CREDITOR

ACCOUNT NUMBER

STARTING BALANCE

CREDIT LIMIT

TARGET PAYOFF DATE

CREDIT TYPE

MINIMUM PAYMENT

INTEREST DATE

DATE	MINIMUM PAYMENT	AMOUNT PAID	BALANCE	NOTES

Debt Tracker

CREDITOR

ACCOUNT NUMBER

STARTING BALANCE

CREDIT LIMIT

TARGET PAYOFF DATE

CREDIT TYPE

MINIMUM PAYMENT

INTEREST DATE

DATE	MINIMUM PAYMENT	AMOUNT PAID	BALANCE	NOTES

Debt Tracker

CREDITOR

ACCOUNT NUMBER

STARTING BALANCE

CREDIT LIMIT

TARGET PAYOFF DATE

CREDIT TYPE

MINIMUM PAYMENT

INTEREST DATE

DATE	MINIMUM PAYMENT	AMOUNT PAID	BALANCE	NOTES

Debt Tracker

CREDITOR

ACCOUNT NUMBER

STARTING BALANCE

CREDIT LIMIT

TARGET PAYOFF DATE

CREDIT TYPE

MINIMUM PAYMENT

INTEREST DATE

DATE	MINIMUM PAYMENT	AMOUNT PAID	BALANCE	NOTES

Debt Tracker

CREDITOR

ACCOUNT NUMBER

STARTING BALANCE

CREDIT LIMIT

TARGET PAYOFF DATE

CREDIT TYPE

MINIMUM PAYMENT

INTEREST DATE

DATE	MINIMUM PAYMENT	AMOUNT PAID	BALANCE	NOTES

Monthly Expense Log

LET'S GET ORGANIZED!

It's time to record my income and manage my other monthly expenses (Utility bills etc.)

Monthly Budget

Income	
Income 1	
Income 2	
Other Income	
Total Income	

Expenses	
Month	
Budget	

Bill To Be Paid	Date Due	Amount	Paid	Note
			☐	
			☐	
			☐	
			☐	
			☐	
			☐	
			☐	
			☐	
			☐	
			☐	
			☐	
			☐	
			☐	
			☐	
			☐	
			☐	
			☐	
			☐	
			☐	
Total				

Monthly Budget

Income		
Income 1		
Income 2		
Other Income		
Total Income		

Expenses	
Month	
Budget	

Bill To Be Paid	Date Due	Amount	Paid	Note
			☐	
			☐	
			☐	
			☐	
			☐	
			☐	
			☐	
			☐	
			☐	
			☐	
			☐	
			☐	
			☐	
			☐	
			☐	
			☐	
			☐	
			☐	
Total				

Monthly Budget

Income		
Income 1		
Income 2		
Other Income		
Total Income		

Expenses	
Month	
Budget	

Bill To Be Paid	Date Due	Amount	Paid	Note
			☐	
			☐	
			☐	
			☐	
			☐	
			☐	
			☐	
			☐	
			☐	
			☐	
			☐	
			☐	
			☐	
			☐	
			☐	
			☐	
			☐	
			☐	
Total				

Monthly Budget

Income		
Income 1		
Income 2		
Other Income		
Total Income		

Expenses	
Month	
Budget	

Bill To Be Paid	Date Due	Amount	Paid	Note
			☐	
			☐	
			☐	
			☐	
			☐	
			☐	
			☐	
			☐	
			☐	
			☐	
			☐	
			☐	
			☐	
			☐	
			☐	
			☐	
			☐	
			☐	
Total				

Monthly Budget

Income		
Income 1		
Income 2		
Other Income		
Total Income		

Expenses	
Month	
Budget	

Bill To Be Paid	Date Due	Amount	Paid	Note
			☐	
			☐	
			☐	
			☐	
			☐	
			☐	
			☐	
			☐	
			☐	
			☐	
			☐	
			☐	
			☐	
			☐	
			☐	
			☐	
			☐	
			☐	
Total				

Monthly Budget

Income		
Income 1		
Income 2		
Other Income		
Total Income		

Expenses	
Month	
Budget	

Bill To Be Paid	Date Due	Amount	Paid	Note
			☐	
			☐	
			☐	
			☐	
			☐	
			☐	
			☐	
			☐	
			☐	
			☐	
			☐	
			☐	
			☐	
			☐	
			☐	
			☐	
			☐	
			☐	
Total				

Monthly Budget

Income	
Income 1	
Income 2	
Other Income	
Total Income	

Expenses	
Month	
Budget	

Bill To Be Paid	Date Due	Amount	Paid	Note
			☐	
			☐	
			☐	
			☐	
			☐	
			☐	
			☐	
			☐	
			☐	
			☐	
			☐	
			☐	
			☐	
			☐	
			☐	
			☐	
			☐	
			☐	
Total				

Monthly Budget

Income	
Income 1	
Income 2	
Other Income	
Total Income	

Expenses	
Month	
Budget	

Bill To Be Paid	Date Due	Amount	Paid	Note
			☐	
			☐	
			☐	
			☐	
			☐	
			☐	
			☐	
			☐	
			☐	
			☐	
			☐	
			☐	
			☐	
			☐	
			☐	
			☐	
			☐	
			☐	
			☐	
Total				

Monthly Budget

Income	
Income 1	
Income 2	
Other Income	
Total Income	

Expenses	
Month	
Budget	

Bill To Be Paid	Date Due	Amount	Paid	Note
			☐	
			☐	
			☐	
			☐	
			☐	
			☐	
			☐	
			☐	
			☐	
			☐	
			☐	
			☐	
			☐	
			☐	
			☐	
			☐	
			☐	
			☐	
			☐	
Total				

Monthly Budget

Income		
Income 1		
Income 2		
Other Income		
Total Income		

Expenses	
Month	
Budget	

Bill To Be Paid	Date Due	Amount	Paid	Note
			☐	
			☐	
			☐	
			☐	
			☐	
			☐	
			☐	
			☐	
			☐	
			☐	
			☐	
			☐	
			☐	
			☐	
			☐	
			☐	
			☐	
			☐	
Total				

Monthly Budget

Income	
Income 1	
Income 2	
Other Income	
Total Income	

Expenses	
Month	
Budget	

Bill To Be Paid	Date Due	Amount	Paid	Note
			☐	
			☐	
			☐	
			☐	
			☐	
			☐	
			☐	
			☐	
			☐	
			☐	
			☐	
			☐	
			☐	
			☐	
			☐	
			☐	
			☐	
			☐	
Total				

Monthly Budget

Income		
Income 1		
Income 2		
Other Income		
Total Income		

Expenses	
Month	
Budget	

Bill To Be Paid	Date Due	Amount	Paid	Note
			☐	
			☐	
			☐	
			☐	
			☐	
			☐	
			☐	
			☐	
			☐	
			☐	
			☐	
			☐	
			☐	
			☐	
			☐	
			☐	
			☐	
			☐	
Total				

My Financial Goals

year:

Finance Goals

What is my ultimate finance goal?

What are the steps that I have to take to achieve my ultimate goal?

The goals for the month of: | Steps

The goals for the month of: | Steps

The goals for the month of: | Steps

year:

Finance Goals

What is my ultimate finance goal?

What are the steps that I have to take to achieve my ultimate goal?

| The goals for the month of: | Steps |

| The goals for the month of: | Steps |

| The goals for the month of: | Steps |

year:

Finance Goals

What is my ultimate finance goal?

What are the steps that I have to take to achieve my ultimate goal?

| The goals for the month of: | Steps |

| The goals for the month of: | Steps |

| The goals for the month of: | Steps |

year:

Finance Goals

What is my ultimate finance goal?

What are the steps that I have to take to achieve my ultimate goal?

The goals for the month of: | **Steps**

The goals for the month of: | **Steps**

The goals for the month of: | **Steps**

Savings Trackers

Saving For

Item	Progress	Amount needed

Saving For

Item	Progress	Amount needed

Item	Progress	Amount needed

No Spend Challenge

year:

| Jan | Feb | Mar | Apr | May | Jun |
| Jul | Aug | Sep | Oct | Nov | Dec |

1 2 3 4 5
6 7 8 9 10
11 12 13 14 15
16 17 18 19 20
21 22 23 24 25
26 27 28 29 30
31

No Spend Challenge

Jan	Feb	Mar	Apr	May	Jun
Jul	Aug	Sep	Oct	Nov	Dec

year:

No Spend Challenge

year:

| Jan | Feb | Mar | Apr | May | Jun |
| Jul | Aug | Sep | Oct | Nov | Dec |

⭐ 1 ⭐ 2 ⭐ 3 ⭐ 4 ⭐ 5

⭐ 6 ⭐ 7 ⭐ 8 ⭐ 9 ⭐ 10

⭐ 11 ⭐ 12 ⭐ 13 ⭐ 14 ⭐ 15

⭐ 16 ⭐ 17 ⭐ 18 ⭐ 19 ⭐ 20

⭐ 21 ⭐ 22 ⭐ 23 ⭐ 24 ⭐ 25

⭐ 26 ⭐ 27 ⭐ 28 ⭐ 29 ⭐ 30

⭐ 31

year:

Savings Tracker

Saving goal

Start date: **Start amount:** **Completion date:**

date	deposited	balance

date	deposited	balance

date	deposited	balance

date	deposited	balance

date	deposited	balance

date	deposited	balance

date	deposited	balance

year:

Savings Tracker

Saving goal

Start date: **Start amount:** **Completion date:**

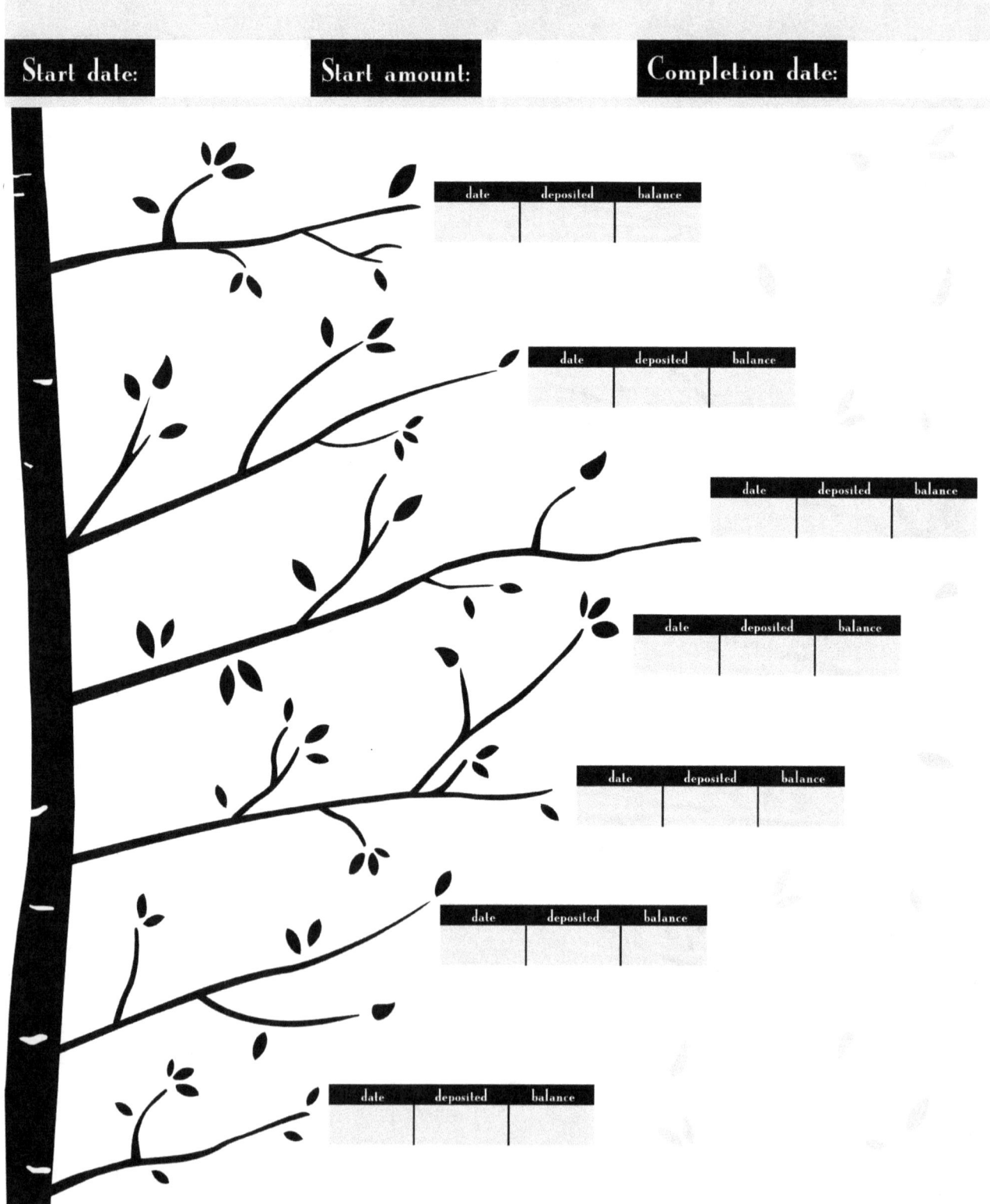

date	deposited	balance

date	deposited	balance

date	deposited	balance

date	deposited	balance

date	deposited	balance

date	deposited	balance

date	deposited	balance

year:

Savings Tracker

Saving goal

Start date: **Start amount:** **Completion date:**

date	deposited	balance

date	deposited	balance

date	deposited	balance

date	deposited	balance

date	deposited	balance

date	deposited	balance

date	deposited	balance

Assets

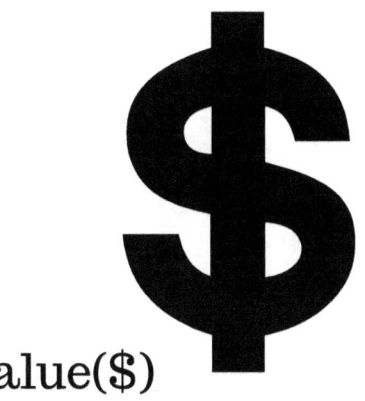

Asset/Description　　　　Value($)

Assets

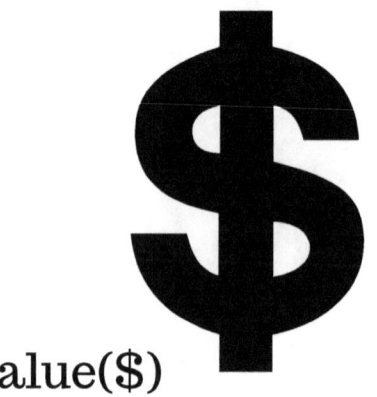

Asset/Description   Value($)

Assets

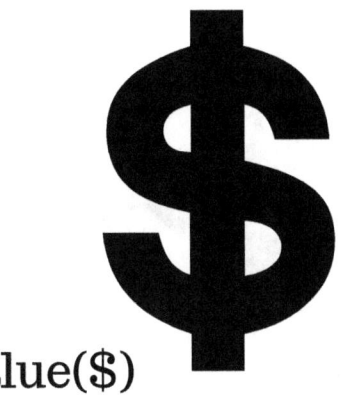

Asset/Description   Value($)

Financial Year in Review

year:

Annual Overview

January
Income:
Expenses:
Savings:

February
Income:
Expenses:
Savings:

March
Income:
Expenses:
Savings:

April
Income:
Expenses:
Savings:

May
Income:
Expenses:
Savings:

June
Income:
Expenses:
Savings:

July
Income:
Expenses:
Savings:

August
Income:
Expenses:
Savings:

September
Income:
Expenses:
Savings:

October
Income:
Expenses:
Savings:

November
Income:
Expenses:
Savings:

December
Income:
Expenses:
Savings:

year: Annual Overview

January
Income:
Expenses:
Savings:

February
Income:
Expenses:
Savings:

March
Income:
Expenses:
Savings:

April
Income:
Expenses:
Savings:

May
Income:
Expenses:
Savings:

June
Income:
Expenses:
Savings:

July
Income:
Expenses:
Savings:

August
Income:
Expenses:
Savings:

September
Income:
Expenses:
Savings:

October
Income:
Expenses:
Savings:

November
Income:
Expenses:
Savings:

December
Income:
Expenses:
Savings:

year:

Annual Overview

January
Income:
Expenses:
Savings:

February
Income:
Expenses:
Savings:

March
Income:
Expenses:
Savings:

April
Income:
Expenses:
Savings:

May
Income:
Expenses:
Savings:

June
Income:
Expenses:
Savings:

July
Income:
Expenses:
Savings:

August
Income:
Expenses:
Savings:

September
Income:
Expenses:
Savings:

October
Income:
Expenses:
Savings:

November
Income:
Expenses:
Savings:

December
Income:
Expenses:
Savings:

year:

Debt name: | Account no.
Starting balance: | Minimum payment:
Goal payoff date: | Interest rate:

Month	Amount	Paid	Balance
January			
February			
March			
April			
May			
June			
July			
August			
September			
October			
November			
December			

Notes

year:

Debt name:

Account no.

Starting balance:

Minimum payment:

Goal payoff date:

Interest rate:

Month	Amount	Paid	Balance
January		☆	
February		☆	
March		☆	
April		☆	
May		☆	
June		☆	
July		☆	
August		☆	
September		☆	
October		☆	
November		☆	
December		☆	

Notes

year:

Debt Tracker

Debt name:

Account no.

Starting balance:

Minimum payment:

Goal payoff date:

Interest rate:

Month	Amount	Paid	Balance
January		☆	
February		☆	
March		☆	
April		☆	
May		☆	
June		☆	
July		☆	
August		☆	
September		☆	
October		☆	
November		☆	
December		☆	

Notes

year:

Debt name:

Account no.

Starting balance:

Minimum payment:

Goal payoff date:

Interest rate:

Month	Amount	Paid	Balance
January	$	☆	$
February	$	☆	$
March	$	☆	$
April	$	☆	$
May	$	☆	$
June	$	☆	$
July	$	☆	$
August	$	☆	$
September	$	☆	$
October	$	☆	$
November	$	☆	$
December	$	☆	$

Notes

year:

Debt name: Account no.

Starting balance: Minimum payment:

Goal payoff date: Interest rate:

Month	Amount	Paid	Balance
January	$	☆	$
February	$	☆	$
March	$	☆	$
April	$	☆	$
May	$	☆	$
June	$	☆	$
July	$	☆	$
August	$	☆	$
September	$	☆	$
October	$	☆	$
November	$	☆	$
December	$	☆	$

Notes

year:

Debt name:

Account no.

Starting balance:

Minimum payment:

Goal payoff date:

Interest rate:

Month	Amount	Paid	Balance
January	$	☆	$
February	$	☆	$
March	$	☆	$
April	$	☆	$
May	$	☆	$
June	$	☆	$
July	$	☆	$
August	$	☆	$
September	$	☆	$
October	$	☆	$
November	$	☆	$
December	$	☆	$

Notes

year:

Debt name:		Account no.	
Starting balance:		Minimum payment:	
Goal payoff date:		Interest rate:	

Month	Amount	Paid	Balance
January	$	☆	$
February	$	☆	$
March	$	☆	$
April	$	☆	$
May	$	☆	$
June	$	☆	$
July	$	☆	$
August	$	☆	$
September	$	☆	$
October	$	☆	$
November	$	☆	$
December	$	☆	$

Notes

year:

Debt name:

Account no.

Starting balance:

Minimum payment:

Goal payoff date:

Interest rate:

Month	Amount	Paid	Balance
January	$	☆	$
February	$	☆	$
March	$	☆	$
April	$	☆	$
May	$	☆	$
June	$	☆	$
July	$	☆	$
August	$	☆	$
September	$	☆	$
October	$	☆	$
November	$	☆	$
December	$	☆	$

Notes

year:

Debt name: | Account no.
Starting balance: | Minimum payment:
Goal payoff date: | Interest rate:

Month	Amount	Paid	Balance
January	$	☆	$
February	$	☆	$
March	$	☆	$
April	$	☆	$
May	$	☆	$
June	$	☆	$
July	$	☆	$
August	$	☆	$
September	$	☆	$
October	$	☆	$
November	$	☆	$
December	$	☆	$

Notes

year:

Debt name: Account no.

Starting balance: Minimum payment:

Goal payoff date: Interest rate:

Month	Amount	Paid	Balance
January	$	☆	$
February	$	☆	$
March	$	☆	$
April	$	☆	$
May	$	☆	$
June	$	☆	$
July	$	☆	$
August	$	☆	$
September	$	☆	$
October	$	☆	$
November	$	☆	$
December	$	☆	$

Notes

year:

Debt Tracker

Debt name: | Account no.
Starting balance: | Minimum payment:
Goal payoff date: | Interest rate:

Month	Amount	Paid	Balance
January	$	☆	$
February	$	☆	$
March	$	☆	$
April	$	☆	$
May	$	☆	$
June	$	☆	$
July	$	☆	$
August	$	☆	$
September	$	☆	$
October	$	☆	$
November	$	☆	$
December	$	☆	$

Notes

Financial Notes

date:

Finance Notes

date:

Finance Notes

date:

Finance Notes

date:

Finance Notes

date:

Finance Notes

date:

Finance Notes

date:

Finance Notes

date:

Finance Notes